# MIRROR MIRROR ON THE WALL

# MIRROR MIRROR ON THE WALL

## Jack Hastie

Cover Design by Mandy Sinclair

Copyright © 2022 Jack Hastie

The moral right of the author has been asserted.

Apart from any fair dealing for the purposes of research or private study, or criticism or review, as permitted under the Copyright, Designs and Patents Act 1988, this publication may only be reproduced, stored or transmitted, in any form or by any means, with the prior permission in writing of the publishers, or in the case of reprographic reproduction in accordance with the terms of licences issued by the Copyright Licensing Agency. Enquiries concerning reproduction outside those terms should be sent to the publishers.

This is a work of fiction. Names, characters, businesses, places, events and incidents are either the products of the author's imagination or used in a fictitious manner. Any resemblance to actual persons, living or dead, or actual events is purely coincidental.

Matador
Unit E2 Airfield Business Park,
Harrison Road, Market Harborough,
Leicestershire. LE16 7UL
Tel: 0116 2792299
Email: books@troubador.co.uk
Web: www.troubador.co.uk/matador
Twitter: @matadorbooks

ISBN 978 1803132 600

British Library Cataloguing in Publication Data.
A catalogue record for this book is available from the British Library.

Printed and bound in the UK by TJ Books Limited, Padstow, Cornwall
Typeset in 11pt Palatino by Troubador Publishing Ltd, Leicester, UK

Matador is an imprint of Troubador Publishing Ltd

*What does he see in the mirror –
a pilgrim? – or a naked ape?*

# CONTENTS

## MIRROR INTRODUCTION

| | |
|---|---|
| On Releasing a Healed Sparrow Hawk | 1 |
| Destiny; a pantoum | 3 |
| Mind Spider | 4 |
| Lost Horizon | 5 |
| Genesis | 7 |
| Shamima | 8 |
| Broaden Your Mind | 10 |

## MIRROR MIRROR ON THE WALL

| | |
|---|---|
| L`Apres Midi d`un Question | 13 |
| The Coin | 14 |
| Autumn (through Chinese eyes) | 15 |
| Moon Landing | 16 |
| Sea Glass | 17 |
| All Hallows Eve | 18 |
| Nirvana | 19 |
| Star Quest | 21 |
| The First Day of Spring | 22 |
| Understone | 23 |
| My Moon | 24 |

## MAGIC MIRROR

| | |
|---|---:|
| Cactus Meadow | 25 |
| Fire Mountain | 26 |
| Over Biscay | 27 |
| The Old Navy Man | 29 |
| Storm | 33 |

## MIRROR FOUR

| | |
|---|---:|
| Lipstick | 36 |
| Freedom | 38 |
| Oak Tree, St. Brelade`s Churchyard, Jersey | 40 |
| Virus | 42 |
| Dream | 44 |
| Id | 46 |
| Infinity | 48 |
| On the Beach | 50 |
| Only a Painting Hanging on a Wall | 52 |

## MIRROR FIVE

| | |
|---|---:|
| An Evening With Beethoven | 54 |
| Resurrection | 60 |
| Inspiration | 61 |

## FINAL THOUGHTS

Haiku Sequence : Homo Sapiens             63

## POSTSCRIPT

On Becoming Eighty Six             65

About the author             67

# MIRROR INTRODUCTION

This short (36 poem) collection is intended to reflect various aspects of my encounter with life.

1 Raw observation eg Sparrow Hawk; Cactus Meadow; Star Quest.

*On Releasing a Healed Sparrow Hawk*

Like a bolt he shot
delta winged
circled the garden low
radar eyes ranging
a stealth bomber.

Then he laughed
and soared
into the high blue heaven
just to show off
all his happiness.

We cheered
and he stooped towards us –
in acknowledgement? Gratitude? –
swivelled
and, with a side stroke of his wings
flipped into a roost
among the leaves of a guardian elm.

2   Abstract intellectual construction eg Destiny; Nirvana; Freedom.

*Destiny; a pantoum*

This cosmos is just space and entropy.
No Godly purpose for the human race.
No working out of holy destiny.
Dead planets orbiting in empty space.

No Godly purpose for the human race.
No prospect of a heavenly escape.
Dead planets orbiting in empty space
With earth the homeland of the naked ape.

No prospect of a heavenly escape.
No working out of holy destiny.
With earth the homeland of the naked ape
This cosmos is just space and entropy.

3   A mixture of each; Mind Spider; All Hallows; Sea Glass.

*Mind Spider*

Why do you skite
your bloated blood-sack
on all those crowding, crooked, crippled claws
that make *my* toes curl
in fright?

Is it to understone
to skulk in shadow
from the smite
of the righteous, cauterising sun?

Why do you crouch each night
always at the edges of my sight
to weave across the corners of my thoughts
webs that snare the flimsy, flickering flight
of all the bright winged butterflies
of my delight?

I know you now!
Your webs crucify the light
bind my mind.

4   Reflections on the writing of poetry: Lost Horizon; The Old Navy Man.

*Lost Horizon*

Wherever I look
an unbroken line, school-boy ruler straight
confronts me
challenges me in its one-ness.

Rising to eye level
always just to eye level
the featureless sea –
no up nor down
no left nor right
colourless as a mirror.
The essence of emptiness.
Planet Lanzarote in a universe of sea.

The line trembles
blurs and melts
slips into mists and hazes.
The anchor is lost.
Shapeless figures loom
merge and dissolve
in that nowhere space
where dreams germinate.

The string twangs taut.
The line is ruler straight again
and real.
I m awake!

*Genesis*

In outer space
a supernova detonates.
Melts your mind.

In your inner space
An archetype mutates.
Rocks your reason.

A poem is born.

5   A few are straight political comment: Shamima; An Evening With Beethoven.

*Shamima*

A flower of fifteen
just a kitten –
but they`d drilled in the dogma:
"The enemies of Islam
must be destroyed."

Forsaking her family
she went, unsheathing her claws:
as Jael to Sisera\*
Judith to Holofernes.\*\*
May Allah be pleased with her.

Now our soft hearts
would fetch her home
(to be lovingly sanitized)
in a specially sealed capsule
like Lenin\*\*\*
transported to Russia –
a toxic plague bacillus.

But what if the capsule
should leak?
Don`t forget Lenin.

- She beheaded a Canaanite general and saved Israel
- She beheaded an Assyrian king and saved Israel.
- Transported by rail in 1917 from Zurich to St Petersburg through German lines.

6   Experimental.

*Broaden Your Mind*

Tingle at the tiptoe
of a midge on your nose.

Taste the sour revenge
of last night`s vindaloo
talking back.

Spot the hoar frost diamond
on a leaf.

Open your eyes
to the incandescent splendour
of a rainbow.

Bathe in the soft, silver slant
of a moonbeam.

Listen for the last sad sigh
of a moth expiring at your window.

Feel the twitch
of a sparrow`s wings
three hedgerows away;

Smell the stink of a skunk
spraying stench in Saskatchewan.

Hear the *kadoof* of a horse`s hoof
rounding a runaway steer
out on the restless prairie.

Confront a charging mammoth
on a glacier.

See those dry bones rise, clothed in flesh:
the T. Rex standing tall.

Stare in wide-eyed wonder
at the dance of many legged things
on Mars.

Glimpse the shadow of a cobweb
trembling in Andromeda*
a million years ago.

★

Endure the fire.
Share Patrick Hamilton`s** agony.

Harken to the scratch, scratch, scratch
of a cockroach
on your grave.

Follow the comets in their orbits.
Calculate the trajectories of the galaxies.

★

Read the mind of God.

★

\*   A spiral nebula; our nearest neighbouring galaxy, millions of light years away.
\*\* Burned at the sake for heresy 1528.

## MIRROR MIRROR ON THE WALL

*L`Apres Midi d`un Question*

In the stun of the sun
even the cicadas cease.
The cypress guard stands at silent attention.

Only the pool
a web of glittering silver
flickers its fairy lights
in this dream-heavy heat.

Among the orange groves
one might meet Pan
smiling as he snoozes
or reaches for his pipes
to spin the sounds
that soothe the world to sleep.

Or Satan!
For this is the beach of Light
Praia de Luz. *

\* From which Madeleine McCann disappeared in 2007.

*The Coin*

This coin in my trouser pocket
is warm as a testicle.
It commands goods and services
and determines disputes with summary procedure –
heads or tails.

Yet it is dead
stamped and congealed with a moment of history
and when the next coin is struck
it will become forgotten history
among the cold exhibits on museum shelves.

With the next generation`s minting
It will retire to be forgotten
among sheaves of documents
in the dusty archives of official records.

*Autumn (through Chinese eyes)*

In the depth of the night
the wind taps out the rhythms of Autumn:
the rain drips, drips;
the hour strikes, strikes.
Birds in their nests feel the coming frost.
Beasts in their dens sense the sunless ice.
In the depth of the night
the flowers will fall asleep.

With whom have I been racing
all those lost weeks and years –
this gallop of light –
for the prize of a straw-yellow beard
and a cracked back?

Half tipsy, I fumble along home.
As the light dies
even my shadow deserts me.

The boat casts off.
As I drift across the line
I steal one last, long look behind.

(Some of the images were suggested by my reading of
Chinese poetry in translation.)

*Moon Landing*

Smiling, sylvan, seductive
with a wink and a hint
Diana will croon
and shimmer you down
in a silver swoon
gliding on one of her beams.

The pock marked calamitous moon
cratered by comets
omen of doom
will lasso you down
to car crash
on a lava dark sea
bereft of breath
and lisp of life.

Once in a while
an Earthling will sail
into orbit
and land with a strike
scoop a handful of dirt
then depart with a jerk
like a dog that`s just pissed
on a dyke.

*Sea Glass*

A sparkling gem stone.
Wandering star of the sea.
Somebody`s rubbish.

Broken beer bottles.
Sharp splinters of smashed jam jars.
A mermaid`s jewels.

*All Hallows Eve*

To-night
all graves gape
all urns open
all requiems are unsaid.

The Eve of All Saints
is all evils` even
and permits the return of the dead
from darkness
curling into light
between suns
in the brightness of night.

Till dawn
like a gong
summons the shades
to their ashes and graves
and like lead
seals them from sight.

## *Nirvana*

Let me be blind
to the geometry of galaxies.
Let me be deaf
to the symphonies of the stars.

Let me be numb
when butterflies and raindrops
trickle little harmonies
across the xylophone of my skin.

Cool my veins.
Damp down my boiling oil of rage
yet warm my wintry mind
and thaw the frozen claw of fear.

Wash my soul
clean of the salt of ecstasy
that makes me clutch at comets` tails.

Suspend me blindfold
in fleshless cyberspace
where there is no light nor dark
heat nor cold
no up nor down
no time.

Liberate my thoughts
from the censorship
of words.

Then let me slip the leash of memory
hate, joy, hunger
heart-beat

so that I can forget to breathe
may fall in love
vanish into love.

*Star Quest*

Have you looked up
on a moon dark night
have you looked up
and swam
with those wandering lights
in their measureless heights
and wondered
who really
I am?

Have you lain down
on a couch reclined
have you lain down
and dreamed
of those gossamer fires
in their gypsy gyres
and pondered
am I
what I have seemed?

*The First Day of Spring*

Today the world is all hooves and wings
and new sounds.

The burn giggles like a girl
awakens the crocus and the chrysalis
quickens the pregnant ewe.

The roll and crash of the ocean
is a symphony
whose allegro shatters pack ice.

Last night
snowbound
I drowsed with a book
on a comfy sofa.

Tomorrow
I`ll dance on a stage
chant for a team
march for a cause.

*Understone*

At noon brightness.
By moonrise the whiteness of night.
How will I hide from this light?

Understone I crouch
all through broad day
concealed by megaliths
from the bright yellow beak of the sun.

My night journeys
are by overshadowed trails.
The swayings of leaves
splash starlight over me
slash me with light.

But always I return to darkness
tunnel into decay.
I batten on hearts
gnaw souls.

## *My Moon*

I dared to stare the moon in the face
last night.
(They said it would be super full.)
But no bright blast of silver blazed
to daze my eyes.

Instead it seem to smile
with just a hint of sadness
as its glances caressed me.
An ashen, sickly, skimmed-milk moon
languishing in pity for me.

# MAGIC MIRROR

The next three poems along with Lost Horizon, were composed during, and on the plane home from a holiday in Lanzarotte.

*Cactus Meadow*

Sterile cinderscape
in a stun of heat.
No moist mole-tunnelled carpet of turf here
and only travesties of trees.
Cacti
arthritic embryos of souls
that might have become
oaks or elms
stunted, deformed
slain by the sun.

*Fire Mountain*

Splendour of desolation.
Misshapen blocks of lava
like the eggs of a monstrous, demented bird.
Brobdignag figures.
A stampede of dinosaurs –
T. Rex and stegosaur
triceratops at bay.
Surely these must have confronted Medusa
In some Gorgon-haunted night.

Devastation of splendour.
Ulcerated surface
pox marked by pustules and weeping sores
where the thin crust of reason
has broken to release
the fury below;
the ID of the planet.

*Over Biscay*

In a place behind the rain clouds
there`s a land of make believe
a landscape of quicksilver
of sparkle and crystal
where golden islands swim towards you
out of a blue haze
and shadowy swimming pools deepen and dissolve.

There`s a wisp of comet`s hair
hanging round me like a veil.
Coils of silver breath fan me
In these cloudscapes of the skies.

A procession of moving pictures glides below me:
rainbow sprays; jewels of silver filigree;
footprints where angels have danced; – here`s a
    horse shoe; a loving heart; a string of pearls;
a giant bear`s paw; the face of a goat, bearded and horned.

Slowly a grey, creeping thing crawls over them
and smears the scenes
turns vomit yellow
as the old sun shoulders himself out of the sky.

At last the skeleton of a horse
drifts before me
cancer grey
as the light dies.

Then, behind me
a full moon rises
to preside over ghosts.

*The Old Navy Man*

He came more like a beggar than a salesman
had written a book
and wondered, was it any good?
Like a bowl, he offered it
for us to drop in – if merited –
some small change of approval.

"What`s it about?" we asked?
"Short stories, sci-fi, children`s verse?"
So he began to talk.
Memories, chasing each others` tails,
scampered round the room
wandered off to doze in corners
and then startled awake again
to scuttle round in repetition.

Not your cheerful fair wind and salt spray stuff
but

Sodomy at sea, and
ashore – the old taunt:
"Someone shagged a sheep."
Churchill piped on board at Scapa Flow.
"He sent two warships to their deaths."*

The loss of the `Repulse` off Singapore.
The staggering
stabbed ship shouldering
over. Overturning.
Men trapped under leaden decks
swallowing the sea.
Cork-like freedom for others, swilling
past the thrash of propeller blades
into shark-calm water.

Photographs
scribbled autographs
of those
only boys
he did not see again.

Patronisingly I said
his stuff was good.
Good!
His lightning sharp images –
The kamikaze pilot –
"He flew down my gun barrel."
His barbaric voices –
The gunner`s scream
"As his death detonated round him."

He seemed pleased.
"What do you write yourself, Jack?"

Suddenly I felt diminished by this man.
Ersatz emotion in poems?
Contrived drama and second hand horror in stories?

Yet he will have to hook up his raw flesh to drain
until, bloodless and bland,
minced and mashed with milk and bread and sugar
like a hamburger,
it will not offend the public`s digestion.
You can always add ketchup to taste.

He walked away
the rum of old voyages in his veins.
His book, a warren of wandering tales
a labyrinth of cul-de-sacs
will never be published.

We *are* published.
Some of us sometimes win prizes.
Generally we re-heat other people's hamburgers –
and squeeze on ketchup to taste.

I, who am not called to be Wilfrid Owen,
felt honoured by this visit
from someone
who had something to say.

But now you must excuse me:
I have to attend to my hamburgers.

\*   In 1941 the battleship Prince of Wales and the battle cruiser Repulse were sent to Singapore without air cover, and were immediately sunk by Japanese air attack. It was rumoured in some quarters that Churchill had deliberately sacrificed the two ships in order to encourage the United States to enter the war. Whether this is true or not, the sacrifice was unnecessary because the Japanese had attacked Pearl Harbour three days earlier.

*Storm*

The forecast was for gale force winds
caused by a low pressure system
pushing eastwards..

I waked to the howl
round the house
of a demon from Hell.

I looked out at the trees
tormented and trashed
tossed like rag dolls
in the jaws
of a monstrous, unearthly wolf.

I stepped out of doors
and was slammed to the ground
by an invisible madman.

The following day it was announced
that the "extreme weather"
had been caused by
an exceptionally active frontal system.

## MIRROR FOUR

The first seven poems were written as part of a multi media project originally inspired by Morag Thow as part of the Lochwinnoch Arts Fest, 2020. Each poem was to be accompanied by a photo/painting and a piece of music. Which medium took precedence and inspired the others was for the writer/artist/musician to decide. In my case I started with a photo, wrote the poem and then decided which piece of music represented the mood of the situation best. Of the seven photos, I took one myself, one was sent to me by my son, Neil, and the other five taken from the archives. The music (eight pieces in all) are all in the public domain, though some are not well known.

*Lipstick*

Hush of the office
heads bowed over trivia
whispered chatter of keyboards
slave fingers
eyes in thrall to screens
minds imprisoned in square spaces
defined by square tiled floors.

Coffee break
giddy dreams of discos
make up, perfume, hairdo
boyfriends.

Late nite club
where one can buy
a drink, a date, a high
or perhaps, just possibly love.

After five
queues, rain, leaky shoes
a bus that did not stop
another day of shadows
but for Angeline
there`s always Friday.

This poem should be accompanied by a photo of an office and by a recording of "Angeline" by The Seekers.

*Freedom*

I try to fly; I stun my skull.
I run a yard and blood my nose.
I seek to leave; there`s no outside.
Freely
I choose to lie on a board
and freely
stare at a distant, faint light
through iron bars.

What do I see
as I peer around in this cage?
A crypt that shrinks around me
till the sides converge
and pinion my arms.
A vault that descends on me
till my jaw is clamped
against my knee.
A tomb that contracts until it fits round me
like a skin
tight to the very tips of my finger nails.
Freely
I wriggle my toes.

This piece should be accompanied by a photo of a prison cell and accompanied by a recording of "Through Falling Snow" by Johan Johansson.

*Oak Tree, St. Brelade's Churchyard, Jersey*

Gigantic, ancient, enduring
the Lord of this place.

A Brobdingnag of a tree
anchored in the earth
by the knuckles of its roots
among the graves.

Contorted branches writhe
wrestling invisible demons
clawing always upwards
imploring
stretching towards the sun.

The soul of all the churchyards
of the world.
A prayer
set in living wood.


This poem should be accompanied by a photo of an oak tree and a recording of the Tannhauser Overture by Wagner.

*Virus*

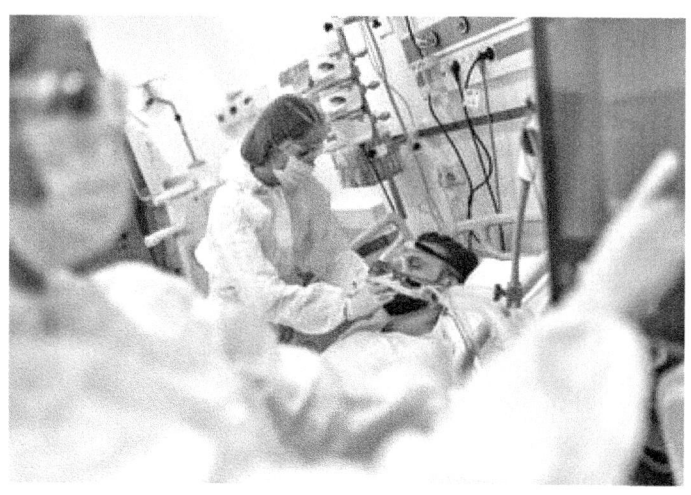

Twist of DNA
that holds the secret of life
yet courier of death
leaping like a dark flame among us
stealing through the interstices of our genes.

The traitor in the handshake
deceiver in the smile
the whisper that breathes
corrosion to our lungs
and ushers us into everlasting night.

Yet turns tail, vanishes
vanquished
in a bowl of soapy water.

This poem should be accompanied by a photo of an intensive care unit and a recording of Grieg`s In the Hall of the Mountain King.

*Dream*

Dream
in this great cavern of Being
this cavern of mind
where we squitter like rats
to find holes to hide.

Listen
to the long hollow, echoing call
of despair.

Dream again.
Shade your eyes
and look up
at the splendour of light
the wildfire, sunburst
the detonation of colour
of brilliance
of beauty.
Gold
always dusting downwards
diminishing
to a touch
a taste on the tongue
a dream of a golden dome.

Then listen again
to the music of a million violins
and soar with it
where arches converge
and parallels meet
An albatross of song.

This poem should be accompanied by a photo of the Aya Sophia as a mosque and by recordings of (1) the Adhan (the Muslim Call to Prayer) and (2) Ave Maria by Maria Callas.

*Id*

In the shadows
from the corner of my eye
leering from the darkness…
No! There`s nothing.

Yet I thought I saw
in the light of an eclipsed moon
the whites of its eyes.
But no! Only the darkness.

The grinning jaws; the crooked teeth.
I must have dosed off
only imagined
the hot stench of its breath
heard
the low hoarse guttural growl.

Tomorrow, at bright sunny smiling noon
I will laugh at myself
tell no one.

But tonight and now
those wolf`s eyes, bloody mouth, panting tongue
summon me
down into the shadows
down, down through the blue-black shadows…

I will remember what I was
I am sick of right and wrong.
I must go back to my real self
and the freedom that was mine.
I will repudiate church and law
the fetters of a will in chains.
and return to my ancient ways
my lost loves and lusts again.

This poem should be accompanied by a photo of a dog
and by a recording of The Beast by Johan Johansson.

*Infinity*

Ponderous, we plod in pilgrimage
from slab to earthbound slab
up granite steps
until
stabbed by the sheerness of the place –
perpendiculars, straight as lances
whispering infinities –
we soar
where planets wheel
and comets glide
and then beyond
to that last abyss
where the thin stars dim
and the galaxies recede
to the last millimetre of measurable space.

There, where number is power
$E = MC^2$
and equations work miracles
a nuclear burst of Being
explodes infinity
and we may at last
all and equally
become gods almighty –
or nothing.

This poem should be accompanied by a photo the interior of Cologne Cathedral and a recording of Nessun Dorma sung by Pavarotti.

*On the Beach*


I squat on the hot sharp sand
of this steep beach
adore the gulls and gannets
wheeling in blue air
that brush blunt earth
only to mock
the multi legged, scuttling, muck-flecked things.
If only my arms were feathered.

The tide`s wide alligator mouth
advances in a rush of waves
a rippling leer of broken teeth.
As the victim sand slurps
I slither, eyes screaming
towards an eyeless, drowned sea-wrack gullet.

The slope is strict
but I brace my heels
dig against the slipping quicksand
implore the gulls
grate back, grinding against gravel.

On the lips of oblivion
I play chess with the flood tide
advance my pieces
empty, mocking cockle shells
vacuous limpets, hollow whelks.

But I`m in an endgame.
Checkmate.
Abruptly
between my toenails
the sea bed capitulates into abyss.
The froth of me
drifts across the face of infinity
dissipating into moon glance and comet shimmer.
I gabble all my wisdom to the gulls
abdicate into – nothingness.

*Only a Painting Hanging on a Wall*

Half asleep
I set aside my crutches
and half forget
all that I have been.
Then, suddenly that painting on the wall
stabs my eye
dynamites my mind.

The savage sea snarls
at the oil-rainbowed, plastic-poisoned foreshore.
The demented sea
curls its slavering lips
bares its foam-flecked teeth
as it tears
raw flesh from the beach.

Far, far out to the high horizon
the great, wild, wandering billows
driven by the winds
drawn by the moon
surge from the unfathomable caverns of the ocean.

In imagination
I am blinded by the spray
deafened by the thunder of the breakers.
On my lips the sting of salt.
The breath of million oceans fills my lungs.

I reach for my crutches
lever myself upright
half awake now, half alive
in the condemned cell of the body –
and I gaze
at this wonderful window on the sea –
and on my past.

I will remember what I was.
I am sick of crutch and pain.
I close my eyes
and in dreams
ride the backs of wild white stallions
wrestle the Pentland Firth in a force nine gale
smell the tang
and tame the sea

once more.

# MIRROR FIVE

*An Evening With Beethoven*

The finale of the overture to Goethe`s Egmont
piles climax on climax
till the last firework explosion
floods the auditorium with a torrent of sound.
With Beethoven`s crashing chords
resounding in their heads
the audience filters
out of the warm stalls and upper circle
shuffles
to cool toilets and cloakrooms
stumbles
down three tiers of frosty, breath stabbing steps
coughing, wheezing
and fans out past Donald Dewar
into the dreich night
to bus stops
train stations
and deserted car parks.

Amrik Singh Surjit
swims with the tide.
An alien tide?
Western music.
Western civilisation?
Widgets and gadgets!!
The rule of law and reason?
Corruption, exploitation!!
David Livingstone, Mary Slessor, Bob Geldof?
Shameless women
bland food
miserable weather!!
Demons slain?
Slavery, suttee, thugee, famine?
The Amritsar massacre.
The white man`s burden?

The steel bracelet
burns on his wrist
reminds him who he is.

Wraiths throng the doubling labyrinth of his mind
dispelling Beethoven

Turbaned warriors.
The Khalsa.
Golden Amritsar
Ranjit Singh, forger of the nation.
Indira Gandhi`s bullet riddled body.
Beant Singh doing what he had to do
kindling a karma of treachery and vengeance
across the memory
of a subcontinent.
And saints
Kabir the poet, mystic;
"I am a child of Allah…and of Ram."

And now Manmohan Singh
the peacemaker.

Amrik slopes off.
His bus behind Saint Enoch Square
is only the length of Buchanan Street
away.

Downhill, beyond halfway,
where The Lighthouse smiles
on Prince`s Square
the City belches.
The pubs are vomiting the faithful
in full song.

Celtic have been plundering Europe
on the box
for Saint Patrick and maudlin martyrdom.
"It`s lonely in the fields of Athenry."

Rangers more aggressively
battling for King Billy (1690)
and The Sash.
"Up to the knees in Fenian blood…"

Match winning goals have pumped high octane levels.
Penalties and sendings off ignited feral bigotries.

Amrik hesitates.
Billy or Pat?
Allah or Ram?
Sunni or Shiah?
Dalit or Brahmin?
Caste damning caste.
Clan killing clan.

The Guru Nanak said,
"There is no Hindu; no Muslim."

"Christ, there`s a fucking Paki.
Away back tae vindaloo
ya poof."

"Gie the black bastard a kicking."
Senga flashes fat thighs
her tits jiggling with excitement.

Thunder of boots.
hail of fists
flailing.
Flash of a lightning blade
(My client carried it
only for protection)
thrust drunkenly
purposefully
ideologically
dogmatically.
White man`s burden?

The sacred black Punjabi beard
drifts like tangled seaweed wrack
in a dribbling Glasgow gutter.
A red stain slithers
like a dying snake
towards Saint Enoch Square
and that bus.

The tight black turban is intact, defiantly.
Protected by Allah
or Ram?
The bright bracelet on his wrist
reminds him who he –
was.

The orchestra packs up.
The dumb instruments slot
into long black silent cases
like coffins.

Egmont was beheaded.
The Netherlands would one day be free
from hate.
One day.

*Resurrection*

Knee on the neck
till the oxygen fails
and all awareness dies.

Chauvin on George Floyd.

Stalin in the gulag;
Hitler at Auschwitz;
bin Laden at a random bus queue;
Ximines and Torquemada
and Calvin exulting, Servetus at the stake:
malignant tumours of humanity.

But there *IS* a resurrection –
though not perhaps for George in person –
for his race – one day;
nor yet for Mother Russia
or those who worship Allah
but, surely, in time –

as there has been for German compassion
and Christian charity.

*Inspiration*

A poem is not an artifact.
You can`t sit down and bake it like a cake
to a recipe
or craft it like a beer
for a market.

From somewhere out in space
it smacks you in the face
and you have to come to terms
with its stun.

It is not an eyewitness account
that you might present in court
where you swear to tell the truth
and nothing but.

The facts are just the ore
you must smelt to find the core
of what they really meant for you
and what you felt.

Thus a gusting force ten gale
is a demon out of Hell
and the image jolts you
once the ore is smelt.

# FINAL THOUGHTS

## *Haiku Sequence : Homo Sapiens*

I am that I am
defined by my NVQ
and P45.

Man views his options
deliberates, makes his moves.
Just like "Battle Chess".*

Made in God`s image.
Lower only than angels.
Man: the naked ape.

I am as I am
spawn of fortuitous genes
and stray DNA.

In love, a poet.
A sage in understanding.
Amps at synapses.**

\*   a chess-playing computer programme.

\*\*  a gap at the end of a neuron that allows an electric current to pass to another neuron.

# POSTSCRIPT

## *On Becoming Eighty Six*

I am tottering
on a shaky step
near the top
of a terrifyingly tall ladder.

Previous steps have lifted me
up through childhood games
adolescent raves and parties
teen romances
to fatherhood
and retirement as a grandpa.

Now
the wind that blows through all eternity
howls around me
and the ladder sways.

Dizzy
I look up
see fleecy clouds
floating in the smile of the sun.

I reach out to touch them
but they swim away
and vanish into distant galaxies
to be swallowed by infinity.

I look down.
On either side
the drop is vast.
I grasp the ladder
till my knuckles turn white.

Sometime soon
I must tread the ladder`s topmost step
in this dreadful sway of the wind.

Then
when I can go no further
lose my grip
and fall

back
through the spool of my life rewinding
till I splash down
somewhere.

# ABOUT THE AUTHOR

Jack Hastie is a retired lecturer in History and an amateur mountaineer. He has published a number of papers on matters of historical interest including "Observations at Kintraw" and "Observing the Moon on the Horizon during the Bronze Age" which deal with archaeo-astronomy, and was a regular contributor to Freethinker Magazine. He is also a regular presenter of as slide-show lecture entitled "From Abu Simbel to Rovaniemi via Akureyri" which is a chronicle of his experiences.

Now he writes mainly poetry and short stories for both adults and children where his grandchildren have been major sources of inspiration. He has written two children`s novels: "Fraser`s Voices" about a Scottish Mowgli who can speak the language of animals and "Neither Dead nor Alive" which is about time travel back to the Bronze Age.

His imagination spans continents and centuries. Never far from his adult writing is an awareness of evil which he sometimes, but not always manages to transcend.

This book is printed on paper from sustainable sources managed under the Forest Stewardship Council (FSC) scheme.

It has been printed in the UK to reduce transportation miles and their impact upon the environment.

For every new title that Matador publishes, we plant a tree to offset $CO_2$, partnering with the More Trees scheme.

For more about how Matador offsets its environmental impact, see www.troubador.co.uk/about/